MW00513233

HANDBOOKS OF EUROPEAN NATIONAL DANCES

EDITED BY
VIOLET ALFORD

DANCES OF FRANCE

I : Brittany and Bourbonnais

Plate I
Baud, Brittany

DANCES of FRANCE

I: Brittany and Bourbonnais

CLAUDIE MARCEL-DUBOIS
and
MARIE MARGUERITE ANDRAL

NOVERRE PRESS

TRANSLATED BY
VIOLET ALFORD
ILLUSTRATED BY
E. JOYCE STONE
ASSISTANT EDITOR
YVONNE MOYSE

First published in 1950
This edition published in 2021 by
The Noverre Press
Southwold House
Isington Road
Binsted
Hampshire
GU34 4PH

ISBN 978-1-914311-06-2

© 2021 The Noverre Press

CONTENTS

Illustrations in Colour, pages 2, 12, 29, 39
Maps of Brittany and Bourbonnais, page 6

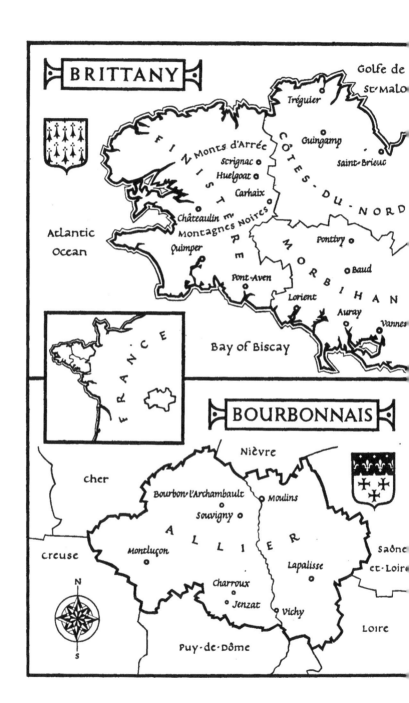

INTRODUCTION

Conditions of living in the old provinces of France established regional differences which the Revolution and its attempts at standardisation were unable to destroy; even the creation of the present departments has so far failed to roll out regional differences to one dead level. Our own subjects—the dances, tunes, instruments and costumes of France—show such surprising diversity that it is intended to present a selection of the most interesting in no less than five sections, grouped in three volumes of this series.

Variety rather than geographical order being our aim, we begin with the North-West, the sea-bound land of Brittany, largely peopled by the descendants of the Cornish fleeing from their own Cornwall to found another Cornouaille across the Channel. With such ancestry we naturally find a special type, a fine local tradition of dance and song, with rich local costumes.

Together with Brittany we present in this handbook a region in the very centre of France, unknown to tourists, half-way between the *langue d'oïl* and the *langue d'oc*, turning its eyes to the south, the old duchy of Bourbonnais. Its costumes are eminently French, so is its music; its Bourrée already in some way smacks of Spain.

In the next volume we go to the Midi, to the old kingdom and province of Provence. Here a different foundation, classic from ancient Greek and Roman days through medieval courts of Provençal kings, produces a culture of its own, a 'polite' rather than a folk culture, compounded of Mediterranean, riverine and Alpine elements.

7

Provence has always been one of the great cross-roads of Europe. Her costumes are Alpine, coastal and urban, the costumes of a highly civilised people. Her dances are chiefly in the same category.

In the same book we shall glance at Alsace, as far removed from Provence in soul as it is in distance. On the eastern confines of France, speaking a Germanic dialect, the Alsatians have led an unquiet frontier life for countless generations and their regional culture shows two main streams. Their costume might be from Central Europe, their Waltz might have come up the Danube and down the Rhine.

In a handbook devoted to the French Pyrenees we hope to give an introduction to the riches of that great chain, containing an unsurpassable variety of dance, costume, language and race. The eastern peaks rise from the Mediterranean, the western from the Atlantic, and between are modern descendants of ancient Gallo-Roman stock. *Fêter, danser*, they say, and there is never a fête without its dance. In French Catalonia are the beginnings of Spanish Catalonia, the same cobla band, the same chain dances and Sardana. In the Central Pyrenees heavy home-woven skirts open out like spinning tops in Bourrée, Castagne and Abricots; the ancient Pyrenean stringed drum beats its accompaniment to a little pipe.

Of the famous Basque dances we shall give no notations. There, woman has little place in fêtes, all is for *Jaun*, her lord and master. In fact she appears just twice in the dance repertory, in the Fandango or Jota—according to which side of the Pyrenees you are—and, almost static, in the chains of Dantza Khorda on the French, and of the Aurresku on the Spanish side. The treasury of Sauts Basques, Soule dances, Sword and Stick dances of the Spanish Basques is for men alone and does not come into the scheme of these handbooks.

The Editor

DANCES OF BRITTANY

BY CLAUDIE MARCEL-DUBOIS

The wide peninsula of Armorica seems a land of ancient magic. Rhythms and movements match the varying colours of the landscape, russet, dark or gay, where the character of the inhabitants too may be rough or friendly. Here korrigans dance round the menhirs, elsewhere the upright stones are girls surprised in their dances and petrified by a curse. Farther on, the souls of wreckers dance a circular procession, solemn and austere; here and there a dance is called 'the Devil's dance'.

We see Bretons dancing at Court in the days of Catherine of Medici (1565), and in the last years of the sixteenth century Henry IV learning the 'passepied de Bretagne'. In the middle of that same century Noël de Fail and Rabelais describe the Triori, the step which is 'à trois pas un saut', requiring many leaps and much suppleness. At this period it was the special dance of Lower Brittany, as against that of Upper Brittany, the Passepied. Madame de Sévigné, who saw the Passepied marvellously performed in Ille-et-Vilaine, writes about their different steps and their cadence, always 'courte et juste'.

The Breton's love of dancing is thus not a modern development. A writer on Breton life in the mid-nineteenth century tells us 'the women share this ardent taste for dancing' but adds, 'the men yell, leap and fling themselves about like madmen' while the women 'are reserved' and view the dance in a 'semi-religious' frame of mind—a memory perhaps of its sacred origin. As for the musicians, the players, the dead themselves would wake and join in, so inspiring is the sound of their biniou and bombarde.

9

Local fêtes, weddings, *pardons*, the end of certain agricultural work, were and still are times for dancing. Certain writers believe they see the last traces of an agricultural rite in such dances as Piler-lan (beating the gorse) or Stoupik (celebrating the last stage of hemp-stripping). A stick or wand dance has been reconstituted in which an ancient Sword dance is thought to live. The Jabadao is supposed to be a memory of the Witches' Sabbath, perhaps the last vestiges of a fertility dance. Certain Rondes (Ring dances) also, such as La Danse de Guisseny or the Jibidi, are supposed to be astral dances.

Although the recreational character of these dances allows no solid foundation for such surmises, they do serve to mark their age-old forms and their oneness with the great family of folk dances which retain the original deep significance of dancing.

Certain Breton dances also have preserved their primitive meaning in a vague memory of their useful and magical purpose. But their symbolism vanished behind their artistic side acquired during long years of give-and-take between country and Court dances. As soon as the isolation of the countryside is broken, exchanges begin and lead according to the times to the development of the Gavotte or the Polka piquée. Later, local tastes modify the form of the once-fashionable dances, which become the personal property of a particular region or a particular group of people. Thus, recently imported dances like the Gymnaska (the only dance in Brittany in six beats*) rub elbows with the most ancient of Midsummer Rounds or agricultural dances.

⁂ ST. JOHN'S EVE AND OTHER OCCASIONS ⁂

These St. John's Eve dances are performed round a fire lit on the gorse-covered commons, or at cross-roads where·

* The rhythm of Breton dances is usually four beats or a multiple of four beats.

large assemblies gather at the winding of horns or the call of the peculiar sound from cauldrons. These cauldrons, in which a little water has been placed, resound through the rubbing of rushes stretched across their orifice which are pulled with the movement used for milking a cow. The water trembles, sometimes the vibration produces an upward spring of a jet of water, and the strange sound can be heard for miles. It is even heard by those of another world, for the souls of the dead come back to warm themselves at the bonfire on Midsummer Eve. Meanwhile, heedless of these unseen visitants, girls who seek a husband jump over the dying flames.

The inauguration of a new threshing-floor is a great occasion for dancing: the more so as by flattening down the soil it serves a useful purpose, the dance being led over the place most in need of treading.

Weddings are the occasion *par excellence*. The procession is hardly out of church before the bride and bridegroom begin to dance. Dancing they go to the banquet with stops at every wine-shop; all that day and for the three following days they dance. The last day—but festivities are shorter now—the poor people of the parish joined with the wedding guests for the ' Gavotte des pauvres '. Formerly the women guests alone performed a dance at the opening of the ball. The bride opened the dance alone, her relations and friends joined in, all without partners, and only after several turns round the dancing-place might the men join them.

REGIONS AND STYLES OF DANCING

Upper Brittany has little by little lost its dances. It is to Lower Brittany (western Brittany, i.e. the west of a line running from Saint-Brieuc to Vannes) that one must go to find dancing; yet even here there are places where the regional dances are beginning to disappear. Groups

Plate 2
Pont-Aven, Brittany

of traditionally-minded Bretons are, however, beginning to dance again. But it is especially in Basse-Cornouaille (Lower Cornouaille), in the mountain district (Montagnes Noires and Monts d'Arrée) and in the Vannetais that dancing remains spontaneous.

Three principal styles have been observed by specialists within the region of Lower Brittany; without excluding the more general characteristic, local temperament and different physical centres have not failed to exert a certain influence upon these various styles.

The Vannetais style (south of Morbihan) is a beautiful poise and simplicity. Arms and legs have an equal share, changes of step are smooth, without complications. Near the sea the dance style is slow and quiet, becoming more lively inland towards Pontivy and the Argoat.

The Hill style is mainly jerky and quick. Towards Châteaulin dancing is sober and ceremonious; in the neighbourhood of Huelgoat and Scrignac the skipping characteristics tend towards the acrobatic. The Piler-lan might be considered as symbolical of the stamping style of the mountains.

In Basse-Cornouaille an opposite style is adopted. Its characteristics are ease, grace and smoothness. This charming style finds its best known expression in the Gavotte of Pont-Aven. It has been said that its movements (amongst which is the celebrated *paz dreo*) imitate the waves by turns undulating, smooth or retiring.

TYPES OF DANCE

Breton dances, like the Breton costumes, are very numerous; only the principal types can be mentioned here.

The Gavotte of Cornouaille, the Ridée of the Vannetais are perhaps the two classical dances of Brittany.

The Breton Gavotte, very different from the Court Gavotte, has two principal forms: the Round, open or closed, often sung in Haute-Cornouaille, and groups of four to the music of biniou and bombarde in Basse-Cornouaille. In the Quimper region it is an honour to lead the Gavotte; in the Argoat all are equal and the leader may not indulge in the fantasies of the Pont-Aven dancer.

The Gavotte is often the first figure of a ' bal ', which is a dance not a ball. There are bals for two and for four in the south of Finistère. In Argoat the bal is simple without repeating the figures.

But everyone best enjoys the wild and gay Jabadao danced all over Cornouaille, beginning with little circles of four to eight dancers, who afterwards form into couples

Amongst the dances more or less connected with agri-culture we will mention the Stoupik (round dance which is danced in short leaps), and the Piler-lan (crushing the gorse, which is used for litter), a dance in two lines, men and women facing each other, the skipping steps of which are characteristic.

The Shepherd's dance of Poullaouen (near Carhaix) is a men's dance, probably belonging to a Christmas mystery play. It is in reality a Passepied. The latter dance is now found throughout the mountain region and occasionally in the Trégorrois.

The Dérobée, danced in 6/8 rhythm in the region of Guingamp, consists of a procession of couples during whose evolutions a partner appears suddenly to steal a lady dancer.

We must also mention the Jibiri, the Gymnaska and those once-fashionable dances now become folk, the Polka piquée, the Avant deux which was a figure of the Quadrille, and the Quadrille itself.

In the Vannetais the most common form is the Round dance. The Tour itself is only a Round dance formerly danced in a ring, instead of in the present form by couples

The Ridée is a Round dance, which sometimes assumes

very large proportions. This name may have been given to the dance either through the words of the refrain '*laride dondaine*', or through its folding-in or wrinkling movements. The Ridée shows variations according to different localities, for example Baud, Auray, Pontivy and so on.

⚜ MUSIC ⚜

Dance tunes are sung, or played by the *sonneurs* on biniou (bagpipe) and bombarde (a rustic oboe). The latter plays the melody, the bagpipe accompanies and acts as the bourdon or drone. The effect is strident, stirring and highly specialised. Formerly a small drum tapped the beat. Traditional dances are always binary in rhythm—except the Gymnaska, which is an imported dance. The airs are simple, usually composed of two fundamental phrases, and always well marked.

⚜ COSTUME ⚜

Pont-Aven. The Sunday costume for young women is marked by the wonderful coif of embroidered linen or lace. A small cap rests on the hair on the top of the head with a pale-blue ribbon round it, itself often covered with fine, transparent lace. Two stiffened wings of lace curve up over the cap to disappear into the top edge of the blue ribbon. Seen sideways these make a figure of 8. The great spreading collar is of goffered linen edged with lace in front and rests on the shoulders like a cape curled up at the edges. The corsage is black or dark-blue with velvet or *passementerie* trimming, wide sleeves heavily embroidered from the elbow down or trimmed with velvet, lace at wrist, and a small white front is worn in the opening of the bodice. A corselet used to be worn, laced in front, but this is obsolescent. The skirt is full round the waist and of satin or silk, but from above the knees to the ankles is of black velvet heavily embroidered. Skirt and corselet are of the same colour as the corsage. A bibbed apron of a pale colour, mainly blue. The embroideries are worked on tulle and sewn on the stuff by appliqué work.

The men wear a black felt hat with broad brim, round the crown a broad velvet ribbon held behind by a silver buckle. The sleeved waistcoat is partly of black cloth, partly of black velvet and has two rows of metal buttons. The jacket or *chupen* is like a sleeveless bolero, of black cloth with stiffened fronts. Some time ago the velvet of these garments was embroidered with two fern-flowers and a cross. The *cor-chupen* is a second little waistcoat but without sleeves, of violet, blue or black cloth, worn over the sleeved waistcoat.

Baud. The women's best dress is black cloth or brocade with velvet trimming and wide sleeves. The skirt is dark and very full; the apron with a small bib is of light-coloured silk; the corselet is square and open in front; a piece of velvet is sewn in the back. Wide bands of velvet slightly gathered on the shoulders fall in front, framing a lace plastron. Above this beautiful dress falls a white lace or net coif like a hood, framing the face and ending behind in a shape like a fish tail. This is called ' queue de raie '.

The men wear a large black felt hat with brim slightly rolled back and a hanging velvet ribbon. The shirt is starched in front.

In both these regions black shoes are worn by men and women.

OCCASIONS WHEN DANCING MAY
BE SEEN

The Sunday before Trinity   Hanvec, Finistère

Midsummer Day, June 24th   Peninsula of Rhuis, Morbihan

First Sunday in July   St-Goazec, Finistère

The Sunday before July 14th   Plogastel, Finistère

July 23rd   Guerlesquin, Finistère

July 31st   Branderiou, Morbihan

August 13th   Penvins-en-Sarzeau, Morbihan

August 28th   Scaër, Finistère

September 4th   St-Eloy, near Hanvec, Finistère

First Sunday in September   Le Faouët, Morbihan

Third Sunday in September   Pont-Aven, Finistère

Last Sunday in September   Plomodiern, Finistère

Certain famous *pardons*—such as Locronan, Auray, Huel-goat, Ste-Anne-la-Palue, Carnac and so on—are the best occasions to see costumes. Some of them end with dancing. They are held in spring and autumn (not during Lent or Advent) on a Tuesday or a Wednesday and last two or three days.

SOME SOCIETIES OF BRETON DANCERS AND MUSICIANS

Fédération des Cercles Celtiques: Loire Inférieure, Côtes-du-Nord, Finistère.

Bodadeg ar Sonerion, Rennes.

Les Fleurs d'Ajonc, Pont-Aven.

Les Bergers, Poullaouen.

Kanfarded, Rosporden.

Les Moutons Blancs, Pontivy.

Nevezadur, Rennes.

Chanterie de Haute-Bretagne, Rennes.

Tréteaux et Terroirs, Nantes.

Societies of Bretons in Paris : Breiz, Cercle Celtique de Paris, Kenvreuriez ar Vinlouerion, Korollerien Breiz Izel.

DANCES OF THE BOURBONNAIS

BY MARIE MARGUERITE ANDRAL

The chaos brought about in France by the Norman in-
asions in the tenth century gave the Dukes of Bourbon
he opportunity to annex parts of the Duchies of Berry,
Auvergne and Autunois. From this new territory was
orn the province which took the name of Bourbonnais
nly in 1327.

This lovely region, lying in the very heart of France on
he border line between the countries of the *langue d'oc*
nd the *langue d'oil*, is now the department of Allier. Its
entle valleys and slopes are planted with vineyards, its
ild spaces covered with heather and broom; mountains
nd deep forests lend beauty to its landscapes.

Its people are carefree and easy-going by nature, and
he art of dancing has always been very highly considered
mongst them. Every Sunday after Mass the young men
nd girls in their Sunday best—which then meant their
wn regional costumes—would dance on the open village
quare, dance halls being quite unknown. They danced
t 'apports', as their fêtes are still called ; during the
ong winter evenings at the veillées, when neighbours
athered for work and amusement at the farms ; and for
edding festivities in the open air or in the barns. Their
ances, though of the same type as those of the neigh-
ouring provinces, have a strong character of their own.
n contrast to the somewhat noisy exuberance of the
Auvergne dances, those of the Bourbonnais invariably
how restraint and a certain melancholy, combined how-
ver with nonchalance which, one can but remark, is
bsolutely in keeping with the regional temperament.

The eighteenth and the beginning of the nineteenth century was the heyday of our dances, and all the effort of the romantic school have not been able to save them from the long decline which has been going on ever since. One must admit that today they are almost completely forgotten.

⚜ TYPES OF DANCES ⚜

The Bourrée. The oldest dance is the Bourrée which, it is claimed, descended from the Gauls. It is entirely different from the too-well-known Bourrée of Auvergne and that of the Limousin. The essential difference is in the rhythm, which is binary instead of ternary as in Auvergne. It is different also in its development and in its figures, different in its character—calm and indolent in place of the liveliness of that of Auvergne. It has always been the favourite dance of one and all, from the young goatherd dancing with bare feet on the grass to Madame de Sévigné who watched it with delight when taking her cures at Vichy or Bourbon-l'Archambault. In the second part of the nineteenth century the Quadrille, then going out of fashion in ball-rooms, became fashionable in the country and superseded the old Bourrée.

The Bourbonnais Polka, the Timb'r and the Cotillon Vert. Other once-fashionable dances appeared too, the Polka Bourbonnaise for instance, a polka but with local variations, changing partners, moulinet figures and so forth. The Timb'r also is nothing but a Polka Piquée, while the Cotillon Vert is partly a Schottische, partly a Valse.

Miming dances. Much more interesting is a series of miming dances, imitating animals: the Chibreli and the Chieb' miming the leaping of goats; the Pas de Loup showing the furtive steps of the wolf; the Moutons, showing in an ever-varying chain formation the confused movements of a flock of sheep. The Chibreli and the Chieb' alone are still danced today.

Wedding Rounds. In the Bourbonnais a peasant wedding is the great occasion for traditional Rondes, ring dances, by all the guests after the banquet. One such Ronde is round a cabbage—a symbol of fecundity—another round a fire on which the hats of the parents-in-law are burning and over which everybody must jump, the bride last in the field.

A RITUAL DANCE

Montluçon possessed an interesting example of that widely spread ritual creature, the hobby-horse. Just as the English hobby-horse at Padstow in Cornwall is said to have been invented ' to frighten off the French ', so this Bourbonnais creature is reputed to have acted against the English when they were defeated in the suburbs of the town. Another version says that a Baron de Montluçon, who had been fighting a neighbouring seigneur, was saved by his horse which magically smelt treachery and returned of its own volition to the battlefield, where the supposedly defeated army was preparing another attack. But more credibly both these are the usual aetiological tales to explain something whose origins are lost in time. In any case the first historical mention of the animal occurs in 1450, when a Fraternity of the Saint-Esprit seems to have taken over the organisation of the fête of the ' Chevau-Fug ', which is hobby-horse in *langue d'oc* —literally a lively or skittish horse. Five of the brethren, dressed in medieval soldiers' costumes, with high pointed head-pieces made of rushes, danced with swords which they ' waved in time to the music '. One fell ' mortally wounded ', others pretended to flee. Another account says a victorious Ronde was danced round the fallen man.

The magical character of the ceremony seems attested by the animal coming out on Whit Monday, a spring festival, and by what sounds uncommonly like a Sword dance. Later the horse was led to church, where he was fed with oats before the High Altar and was made to drink from the Holy Water stoup. His fraternity ended the proceedings by a feast—the whole a nice example of the Christian Church taking a pagan creature under its generous wing.

⚘ MUSIC ⚘

Barrels are rolled on to the *place* or set up in the barn. On these climb the *maîtres sonneurs*, the master musicians who direct the ball. They are greatly admired and respected; some have become quite famous like the legendary Marquis de Beaucaire, a *sonneur* who is remembered still. The vielle (hurdy-gurdy) and the bagpipe strike up and the sabots around begin to mark the steps. The bagpipe or *musette* is composed of a bag of goat-skin, two bourdon pipes and the treble pipe played with both hands. The vielle, so ancient an instrument that it is mentioned already in the tenth century, has held an important place through the Middle Ages, was neglected during the Renaissance and seventeenth century, and came back to favour in the eighteenth, when it even appeared at Court. Now it is again a rustic instrument, and not only played but made in the Bourbonnais. In two villages, Charroux and Jenzat near Vichy, are celebrated musician families, who from father to son devote their lives to the making of these vielles—' the best that ever were ', so the players say. In the workshop of his forefathers, a young Pajot still makes his instruments and is teaching his son to follow in his steps. It is somewhat like a deeply bellied viol; the strings are vibrated by a wheel turned by a handle on one side of the instrument. The *chanterelles*, that is to say the two strings which give the melody, are not played by the hand but by keys as on a piano keyboard. Four more strings give the bourdon, and as a rule the vielle is tuned to D. This explains why practically all the dance airs are found originally written in that key.

✣ COSTUME ✣

'*Bourbonnais, bourbonnichon,*
Habit de velours, ventre de son ! '

The Bourbonnais men and women have the reputation of being vain and coquettish and of thinking overmuch of their appearance, more especially when going to dance. In the women's costumes only the head-dress varies from region to region. Moulins, Souvigny, Bourbon-l'Archambault and their districts are the homes of the famous hat ' à deux bonjours '. It is a straw hat trimmed with black velvet ribbon and straw ornaments. Its large brim is tilted up in front to frame the face. This is the ' bonjour de devant '. At the back, slightly smaller, is a similar brim, the ' bonjour de derrière '. It is lined with red silk for girls and young women, with blue silk for older women and widows. It is worn over a white embroidered cap with two crimped frills encircling the face. The western region prefers the ' quichenotte ' (kiss-not) of a simplified shape, also made of straw, the black velvet ribbons crossed round the crown and falling on the shoulders.

Montluçon and its district possess a lovely cap richly embroidered, trimmed with wide Valenciennes lace and bright ribbons. It is kept in place by two gold pins joined by a slender chain.

A much gathered petticoat holds out the skirt, itself very full with big gathers all at the back, made of plain or striped material of dullish colours. The bodice is tight-fitting, buttoned up the front and with long, tight sleeves. A bibbed black apron is pinned to the bodice and tied round the waist. Often a bright fichu is worn on the shoulders, of linen or cotton, pointed at the back and crossed under the bib of the apron. Stockings are white, sabots are varnished and have upturned toes and a little decorated leathern strap over the instep.

A heavy cape of *droguet* (a mixture of hemp and wool)

23

keeps the wearer warm, for which a lovely Indian shawl
is substituted on fête days.

Men wear a short brown or black coat, cut with basques,
fitting at the waist and with wide revers, a waistcoat of
a livelier colour also with wide revers, black cloth ' flap '
trousers. The shirt is white, with a high collar; a bright
tie goes twice round the neck to tie in front in a bow.

TWO FAMOUS FÊTES

April 23rd   Saint-Georget (St. George), patron of the
vines at Désertines and around Mont-
luçon. Processions and invocations to the
Saint.

November 11th Sainte-Marion. Pilgrimage near Montluçon to seek a husband during the same
year.

✻ NOTE ✻

*The best-known of the French regional costumes are certainly
those of Brittany. Each district has its own, distinctive in cut,
head-dress and embroideries. The men's hats also are distinct.
Do not talk of ' the ' Breton costume but of the costume of Pont-
Aven, of Baud and of other regions. The dresses of the Bourbonnais are eminently French, simple and elegant, but do not be
tempted to think these ' will do ' for dances of Brittany.*

The Editor

THE DANCES

TECHNICAL EDITORS
MURIEL WEBSTER AND KATHLEEN P. TUCK

༷ଈ

ABBREVIATIONS
USED IN DESCRIPTION OF STEPS AND DANCES

r—right⎫ referring to   R—right⎫ describing turns or
l—left ⎭ hand, foot, etc.   L—left ⎭ ground pattern

C—clockwise   C-C—counter-clockwise

For descriptions of foot positions and explanations of any ballet terms the following books are suggested for reference:

A Primer of Classical Ballet (Cecchetti method). Cyril Beaumont.

First Steps (R.A.D.). Ruth French and Felix Demery.

The Ballet Lover's Pocket Book. Kay Ambrose.

Reference books for description of figures:

The Scottish Country Dance Society's Publications. Many volumes, from Thornhill, Cairnmuir Road, Edinburgh 12.

The English Folk Dance and Song Society's Publications. Cecil Sharp House, 2 Regent's Park Road, London, N.W.1.

The Country Dance Book I-VI. Cecil J. Sharp. Novello & Co., London.

POISE OF THE BODY AND HOLDS

BRITTANY

The poise of the body should be natural and easy. Dancers may link arm-in-arm or join with little fingers linked and hands shoulder-high as in the Gavotte de Pont-Aven or the Ridée de Baud. Occasionally the arms (slightly bent at the elbow) move forward and backward, but more often the dancers are tightly linked arm in arm.

BOURBONNAIS

The Bourbonnais style is graceful and somewhat indolent. The Pas de Bourrée demands a swaying turn of the shoulders following the advancing foot, strongly reminiscent of a Portuguese Vira movement, as described in *Dances of Portugal* in this series. When dancing alone, the men may place their hands on their hips, the women may hold their skirts.

BASIC STEPS

BRITTANY

Breton dancers raise the free foot well off the ground behind, bending the knee. (Do not exaggerate this characteristic.)

	Beats
Paz Dreo	
Pass the r foot behind the l, describing a semi-circle in the air in so doing. (See Gavotte de Pont-Aven.)	I

Pas de Bourrée	Beats
l foot forward.	1
Glide pointed r foot alongside of l foot.	2
Tap the r heel forward on the ground.	1
Jump in place on the r foot, the l foot raised (this entails using the r foot three times running).	2
Step back on the l foot.	1
Glide pointed r foot alongside of l foot.	2
Tap the r heel on the ground behind.	1
Jump in place on the r foot, raising the l foot.	2

(One whole step takes 4 bars.)

The swaying Vira-like shoulder movement is very marked as the dancers move forward and backward. This step is not an easy one. It should be practised forward and back until quite automatic before attempting to acquire the swing of the shoulders.

Balancé (Bourrée)	
Step sideways to the L with l foot.	1
Hop on l foot.	2
Step sideways to the R with r foot.	1
Hop on r foot.	2

Chassé	
l foot upward and forward.	1
Close r foot to l foot.	and
l foot forward.	2
Repeat, stepping forward with r foot.	(*1 bar*)

Pas Sauté (La Chieb')
  Spring on to l foot, throwing the r leg for-   I
  ward.
  Repeat, but spring on to r foot.   2
  Repeat, using alternate feet for each spring.   (*2 steps*
                                                   to each
                                                   bar)

GAVOTTE DE PONT-AVEN

Region   Pont-Aven, Brittany.

Character Fresh and gay but dignified.

Formation In lines of four composed of two couples, each
            group being called a Quadrette. The dancers
            stand close together with arms linked and
            hands held firmly. The men are on the out-
            side and the women on the inside of each
            line. The left-hand man is the leader and is
            called Chevalier de Tête. He is the best dancer
            and may execute fancy movements, sometimes

Plate 3
Bourbonnais: Moulins, Souvigny and Bourbon-l'Archambault

letting go of his partner's hand to turn on his own axis. These fantasies may be danced by the whole Quadrette. On a signal from the leader they may all drop hands and turn half-way round to face the opposite direction. The other man, now on L, becomes the leader. After the start, in which the line should move obliquely to the L, the Chevalier de Tête leads as he likes in a series of curves rather like a Farandole, but whatever the dancers do the rhythm of the dance must continue unchanged.

Dance	MUSIC
Start feet together. Only one step is used and takes eight beats of music. This step is then repeated throughout the dance.	
	Half-bar
1 **Step** forward on l foot.	beat 2
	Bar 1
2 Step forward on r foot.	beats: 1
3 Step forward on l foot.	2
	Bar 2
4 Hop on l foot with r foot raised in front.	beats: 1
5 Pass the r foot (describing a semi-circle with it) behind the l foot (Paz dreo).	2
	Bar 3
6 Step forward on l foot.	beats: 1
7 Step forward on r foot.	2
	Bar 4
8 Hop on r foot with l foot raised in front.	beat 1
Repeat this step, beginning with step forward on l foot on beat 2 of bar 4.	

GAVOTTE DE PONT-AVEN

Air 'Ar Pillaouer' (Le Chiffonnier)
Arranged by Arnold Foster

Allegro vivace ♩ = 152

RIDÉE DE BAUD

Region   The Vannetais, Brittany.

Character   Gay and flowing. The swinging of the arms adds to the interest and movement.

Formation   A circle moving C, men and women standing alternately with little fingers linked, arms forward, hands shoulder-high.

Dance	MUSIC
Feet together, toes to centre. Only one step is used, which takes eight beats of music. This step is then repeated throughout the dance.	
	Bar 1
1 Step on to r foot, passing it across and in front of l foot; at the same time swing the arms backwards and downwards.	beats: 1
2 Step to L with l foot, swinging the arms forwards and upwards.	2
	Bar 2
3 Close r foot to l foot, swinging the arms backwards.	beats: 1
4 Step to L side with l foot.	2
	Bar 3
5 Point r foot forward and rest on r heel.	beats: 1
6 Bring r foot to side of l foot.	2
	Bar 4
7 Hop on r foot with l foot raised.	beats: 1
8 Step sideways to L with l foot.	2

RIDÉE DE BAUD

From the Vannetais
Arranged by Arnold Foster

During bar 4 the arms move quickly down-ward; then as quickly upward to shoulder height.

Repeat as often as desired but always moving C.
The tune may be sung as well as played by the bombarde and biniou.

LA CHIEB' (La Chèvre—The Goat)

Region Chiefly round Bourbon–l'Archambault, Bour
bonnais.

Character Gay; in the character of a Jig.

Formation Couple dance. Partners stand vis-à-vis with
hands on hips.

Dance	MUSIC
The Pas Sauté is used throughout the dance —two steps to each bar of music.	Bars
1 16 pas sautés, starting by springing on to the l foot and throwing the r foot forward and upward.	A 1–8
2 Partners link r arms and turn C on the spot with 8 pas sautés.	B 9–12
3 Turn quickly and link l arms and take 7 pas sautés on spot, but moving C-C to end in place.	C 13–15
Stand vis-à-vis with hands on hips to repeat.	16
Repeat as often as desired, quickening the pace each time.	

LA CHIEB'

From the Bourbonnais
Arranged by Arnold Foster

The tunes of the Breton dances are played on the bombarde and the biniou and those of the dances of the Bourbonnais on the vielle. For practical use, however, piano accompaniments have been added to the melodies noted by the authors.

LA BOURRÉE BOURBONNAISE

Region   Everywhere in the Bourbonnais.

Formation   Groups of at least four couples. Partners stand vis-à-vis in two lines, about 2 yards apart, as in a longways Country Dance.

Character   Smoothly and with a somewhat indolent air.

Dance

Before starting the dance the musicians play an opening called 'Le Didou', during which the men, hats in hands, bow to their partners, kiss them on both cheeks, and then step back to their places in the line.

The men start the dance, moving towards their partners to take them by the hand and lead them into the dance. On bar 3 of A music, the women move forward as the men move backward with the second part of the step.

1 *Pas de Bourrée* (see Basic Steps) This movement goes forward and backward: the Pas de Bourrée is repeated 4 times altogether by the men, each Pas de Bourrée taking 4 bars of music. The women, entering the dance on bar 3, will therefore only do the step 3½ times.

MUSIC
Bars
'Le Didou' repeated 4 times or more

A
1–16

36

BOURRÉE BOURBONNAISE

Arranged by Arnold Foster

2 *Balancé* (see Basic Steps)	B
This is danced on the spot and vis-à-vis with partner.	17
Step to side on l foot.	(beat 1)
Hop on l foot.	(beat 2)
Repeat from side to side three more times.	18–20
3 *Croisé*	C
Partners cross to each other's places, passing r shoulders and using chassé steps, one to each bar of music.	21–24
4 *Balancé*	D
Repeat movements of 2.	25–28
5 *Croisé*	E
Repeat movements of 3. End in own places to begin again and repeat the dance as often as desired.	29–32

Plate 4
Bourbonnais: Montluçon region

BIBLIOGRAPHY

꿍꿍 ᐟᐟᐟ 꿍꿍

BRITTANY

ANTHONY, JEAN.—*Contribution à l'étude du folklore breton: Danses de Basse-Bretagne*. Rennes, 1942.

AUBER, O. L.—*Les Costumes bretons*. Saint-Brieuc, n.d.

BOURGEOIS, ALFRED.—*Recueil d'airs de biniou et bombarde*. Rennes, 1897.

GALBRUN, ERWANEZ.—*La Danse bretonne*. Carhaix, 1936.

MARCEL-DUBOIS, C.—*Documents musicaux bas-bretons (mission 1939)*. Paris, 1943. (MS. in the Musée des Arts et Traditions Populaires, Paris.)

PERRIN ET BOUET.—*Galerie bretonne, Breiz Izel*. 3rd ed. Paris, 1856.

QUELLIEN, N.—*Chansons et danses des Bretons*. Paris, 1889.

RECORDS: A list of commercial records of bombarde and biniou (Pathé, Grammont, etc.) is kept in the Discothèque of the Musée des Arts et Traditions Populaires, Palais Chaillot, Place du Trocadéro, Paris, which also contains an important collection of original records of dance tunes and folk-songs from Cornouaille and the Vannetais, recorded in 1939 and 1943 during the researches undertaken by the Musée.

BOURBONNAIS

ALLIER, ACHILLE.—*L'Ancien Bourbonnais*. New ed. Moulins, 1934.

BLANCHARD, ROGER.—*Les Danses du Limousin et des régions avoisinantes*. Paris, 1943.

JANIN, E.—*Histoire de Montluçon*. Montluçon, 1904.

NORE, ALFRED DE.—*Coutumes, mythes et traditions des provinces de France*. Paris, 1846.

PAULY, E.—*Les Brayauds de Combrailles*. Moulins, 1936.

PRADEL, G.—*La Vielle*. Paris, 1930.

VIPLE, JOSEPH.—*Histoire du Bourbonnais*. Moulins, 1923.

CPSIA information can be obtained
at www.ICGtesting.com
Printed in the USA
LVHW011305260623
750799LV00001B/6